LIBERTY LANE

A BALLAD PLAY OF DUBLIN
IN TWO ACTS WITH A PROLOGUE
BY AUSTIN CLARKE

DOLMEN EDITIONS XXVII

© 1978 Nora Clarke

ISBN 0 85105 324 6

All enquiries regarding performing and other rights
should be made to the Permissions Department,
The Dolmen Press Limited,
The Lodge, Mountrath, Portlaoise, Ireland.

Printed in Ireland

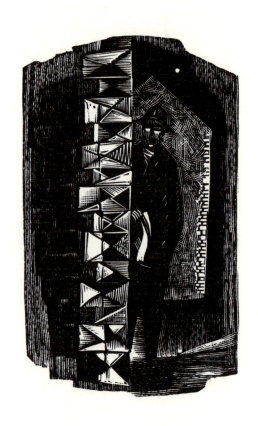

AUTHOR'S NOTE

THE *late F. R. Higgins was the first to write a verse drama about Dublin's 'low-life'. A Deuce of Jacks was based on an anecdote about Michael Moran, better known as Zozimus, a ballad-maker, in the early part of the last century, which tells how some practical jokers held a mock wake for him. This one-act play, written in a vigorous, irregular measure, was produced at the Abbey Theatre and might have been a success but for the unsatisfactory ending. Later, it was printed in* The Dublin Magazine.

During many years, I thought over the play and when I had learned more about dramatic technique, I ventured to make some changes in the last scene, in the hope that these would render it effective. The Lyric Theatre Company, founded in order to maintain the new movement in verse drama, offered to hire the Abbey Theatre and give several Sunday performances of the amended play, but failed to obtain permission from the Literary Executor.

Eventually, I could not resist adding to the new ending my own version of the traditional story.

Austin Clarke

NOTES ON THE TEXT

Ballads of Zozimus : *Ballad of Donnybrook Fair.* Attributed by the late D. J. O'Donoghue to a journalist of the time. An interesting example of the wheel-and-bob stanza.

Swift : from *Epilogue to a Play for the Benefit of the Weavers in Ireland.* 1721.

O'Rourke's Feast. This translation appeared in a volume of mine entitled *Flight to Africa.*

LIBERTY LANE

CHARACTERS

THE PROLOGUE

MR EDWARD CARSON
CAPTAIN TERENCE O'NEILL
MARTIN McGUCKIN
MR TITMARSH
MR CHARLES LEVER
A Waiter

THE PLAY

PATRICK DELANEY
MARTIN McGUCKIN
ZOZIMUS
MR WILLIAM BROWNE
MR DENIS CLARKE
FATHER SULPICIUS
KEARNEY, *a ballad singer*
O'LEARY, *a ballad singer*
MAGRANE, *a ballad singer*
HUMPY SODLUM
GORT WHELAN
COLLEEN OGE
BILLY BOLAND
MRS LISA BOLAND

MRS NELL FLAHERTY
MRS HANNIGAN
THE TOUCHER MAGUIRE
NOBS FAHY
PHELIM BRADY
FRED FURY
MIKE MYLER
BRIAN O'LYNN
BIG JIM PLANT
MOLLIE MALONE
MRS MULLIGAN
DAN KENNY
DANIEL O'ROURKE
DERBY DOYLE

Actors and Others

PROLOGUE

(*A private lounge in the Shelbourne Hotel, Dublin. Left, small screen, Mr Titmarsh writing at a desk. Two long windows at back. Voice of a fishwife: 'Dublin Bay Herrings! Dublin Bay Herrings!'*)

MR CARSON
   What will you have, Captain O'Neill?

CAPT O'NEILL   The old
   Reliable.

MR CARSON   I'll pull the bell-rope.
                                          As I
   Was saying, I opened *The Freeman's Journal* at the
      second
   Page, column three, this morning. What do you think
   I read?
            A new subscription for a statue
   Of Father Matthew, to be executed as soon as
   He shines above.

CAPT O'NEILL   Too many flies on that ceiling!

(*waiter enters*)

MR CARSON   Good morning, John.

WAITER   Fine morning, Sir.

MR CARSON   Two balls
   O' malt, please.

(*waiter leaves*)

                    Think of it. Monster meetings
In field or market town, from Skibbereen to,
Say, Smithfield. Populace taking the pledge, hands up
To Heaven. And the result — the public-houses
Empty.

CAPT O'NEILL   Cart-horses pulling up and looking
Surprised when they get a 'Go wan ow a' that!'
                                   from their driver
And a flick of unwilling whip.

(*waiter returns*)

MR CARSON   Thanks, John.

(*waiter ready with water-jug*)

                    The same as usual.

(*waiter leaves*)

                                   The banks
Foreclose and twenty thousand people —

CAPT O'NEILL   That's
   So.

MR CARSON   Emigrate to Liverpool, fare paid, with
   Their kith and kin.

CAPT O'NEILL   Steam-packets, stokers, busy.

MR CARSON (*raising glass*)
   And now the emancipated are cheering themselves
   Like us.

CAPT O'NEILL   Pledging to take the pledge again
   Next Lent.

MR CARSON   The country is going to the bad.
   The very potatoes are rotting.
                    And now young Davis —

I knew his father when he lived in Baggot Street —
Wants Catholic, Protestant, to unite. It's worse than
Repeal.

CAPT O'NEILL   Well, I'm a Presbyterian, as
You know. My father carried a long pike
In '98 and wore the Green in Antrim
Town.

MR CARSON (*admiring*)
Yes, but his son has a British uniform —

CAPT O'NEILL (*smiling*)
Not hidden in a hayloft!

MR CARSON (*lowering voice*)   Are you a Mason?
(*the other shakes head*)
I'll nominate you.

CAPT O'NEILL (*laughing*)   Did you ride the buck-goat?
At midnight in Molesworth Street, Mr Carsoni —
Sorry, I meant . . . er . . . Mr Carson.

MR CARSON (*offended*)   Sir.

CAPT O'NEILL   Only a joke.
(*gets up, looks out of window*)
                              — and talking of jokes, there's
Martin McGuckin, hurrying to the Hotel.

MR CARSON   The actor?

CAPT O'NEILL   And party impersonator, last of the rakes,
Relative of Sir Joshua Barrington.
Drink up your whiskey, Mr Carson, or he'll sword-
    stick
You for a sovereign from your fob. He's playing
A practical joke for a bet, to-night in the Coombe —

A dangerous spot — and the odds are against his
    keeping
A dirty shirt on his back or his cranium
Uncracked. Last Monday, he challenged me at the Club
And in a trice my pocket had been *touché*.

(*They hurry out. Mr Martin McGuckin enters.
Followed by waiter with tray.*)

WAITER   Your ball o' malt, Mr McG.

MR McGUCKIN   Good! Don't drown
'The poor craytur', Johnnie.
              Leave a few shamrocks floating
On it.
(*Waiter leaves. McGuckin comes forward, recites in
flat Dublin accent.*)
At the dirty end of Dirty Lane
Lived a dirty Cobbler, Dick McClane;
His wife was, in the old King's reign,
A stout brave orange-woman.
(*glances at broadsheet*)
On Essex Bridge she strained her throat
And six-a-penny was her note.
But Dickey . . .
(*hears a cough, turns, sees Mr Titmarsh at door*)
Excuse me, Sir, I didn't see you at all.
A stranger to this country?

MR TITMARSH   Yes, English. On
A visit. My name is Titmarsh.

MR McGUCKIN   Mine's McGuckin.
Pleasure to meet you, Sir.

MR TITMARSH   I couldn't help hearing
    Your ballad.

MR McGUCKIN   Not mine, Sir. It's by Zozimus,
    Our Dublin street-bard, our blind Homer come
    To his last city.

MR TITMARSH   What a strange name he has!
    It's not quite Irish!

MR McGUCKIN   He earned it, penny by penny,
    With a hymn he composed about a forgotten Pope
    Called Zozimus, who lived in the fourth century
    And converted —
    (*lowering voice*)   a fallen woman.

MR TITMARSH   Curiously
    Enough, I've been writing a ballad, too, entitled . . .
    Er . . . *Mr Maloney's Account of the Ball*. I'm trying
    A bit o' the brogue.
    (*McGuckin shows alarm*)

MR TITMARSH (*smiling*)   It's not finished yet.

MR McGUCKIN (*hastily*)
    Goodbye, Sir.
                     Bianconi will wrap you in his
    New waterproofs, the cadgers and 'childer' beat
    His chargers to the canal-boat.
                                And don't forget
    To visit Blarney Castle.
    (*looking in again*)
                        I come from there.

(*Mr Titmarsh comes forward with paper and tries to
recite in a thick brogue*)

MR TITMARSH
> Begor this fête all balls does bate
> > At which I've worn a pump and I
> Must here relate the splendour great
> > Of the Oriental Emperor.
>
> There was Baroness Brunser that looked like Juno,
> > And Baroness Rehausen there,
> And Countess Rouiller who looked peculiar,
> > Well, in her robes of gauze in there.
>
> There was Lord Crowhurst (I knew him first
> > When only Mr Pips he was)
> And Mick O'Toole, the great big fool
> > That after supper tipsy was.
>
> There was Lord Fingall with his ladies all
> > And Lord Kileen and Dufferin
> And Paddy Fife with his fat wife:
> > I wonder . . .
> > > > gruffer . . . rougher . . . puff-her, in . . .
> > I wonder how . . .

(*Charles Lever, who has entered quietly, supplies the rhyme.*)

MR LEVER   I wonder how he could stuff her in.

MR TITMARSH   Lever, begad.
> (*they shake hands*)
> > > You're welcome as the Muse in
> Her peplos.
> > > Thanks, I'll dedicate my new
> Book, *Irish Travel Sketches*, to you.

MR LEVER   I'll be
> Much honoured, Thackeray.

                                    I just called in
To invite you for dinner at my place in Templeogue
This evening: carriage outside the Shelbourne here
At six —
                    and bring Maloney with you, of course.

THACKERAY   Delighted!

MR LEVER (*smiling*)
    Has Mr Titmarsh found much by the Liffey-side
    For pen and crayon?

THACKERAY   Rags and robes.
                                    I saw the
    Right Honourable Lord Mayor, Mr O'Connell
    Among his Councillors in a black-oak Parlour
    At a dingy green-baize table, in crimson robes
    With sable collar, white satin bows, cocked hat —
    Black as a lunar eclipse in a pale sky!

MR LEVER   She's back again.

THACKERAY   Who?

MR LEVER   The Comic Muse.

THACKERAY   Then, the Abbey
    Street Theatre, last evening, stage-Irish farce,
    No . . . 'pathriotic draama.'
                                    And you?

MR LEVER   Toppin'
    The marnin', brothing the bhoys!
                                Charles O'Malley,
    Rechristened Tom Bourke, still gallivanting, drinking,
    Quadrilling, tasting a kiss behind a fan that
    Stops feathering — and pure as the celibates
    In their new Government-granted College at
    Maynooth.

14

THACKERAY
            Think, my dear Lever, of our own licentious
      Old Masters.

MR LEVER   Sterne.

THACKERAY   Fielding.

MR LEVER   Smollet.

THACKERAY   And poor Dickens
      Now, keeping the tester curtains drawn.
      (*waiter enters*)
                                    Forgive
      Me. What will you have?
                        No, I insist.

MR LEVER   A drop
      O' whiskey.

THACKERAY   Waiter!

WAITER   Yes, Sir.

THACKERAY   Two balls o' malt,
      Please.

(*Charles Lever and waiter both look surprised*)

            CURTAIN

ACT ONE

(A disused marine stores in Liberty Lane. Table with bottles on right, small casks. In left recess, a rigged bed, stools. Entrance right, up a few steps. Exit, left.)

PAT DELANEY
> Please hurry now, Mr McGuckin, it's a quarter
> Past eight and you must have gargled
> Six chasers of seven-year-old to a quart
> O' plain. So be on your guard
>
> To-night.
> *(Church bells. McGuckin looks puzzled.)*
> > That's the carry-on at St Patrick's.
> Soon the boys will be here for a stiffener
> An' if they get wind of your play-acting tricks,
> There'll be another stiff
> On the slab to-morrow.

McGUCKIN *(with broken bit of mirror)*
> Just one more touch
> Of grease-paint.
> > 'Me gob' is too red.
> More flour.
> *(Delaney hands it to him)*
> > Thanks, Pat.
> > > I must look touching.
>
> For the wake . . .
> *(claps on wig)*
> > And now I'm ready.

DELANEY   Bejases, you're the living dead spit o'
> The corpse of Zozimus

16

Some day in Mercer Street Hospital,
    Penny-eyed, completely unsozzled.

You worked like a Trojan at his whiskers.
(*bitterly*) Poet, my foot! I'll give him more digs
In the ribs for he cheated me, guzzled my whiskey
    An' got me thrun out of my digs.

There's a jar on the shelf near the bolster.

McGUCKIN   Not yet. I need a rehearsal
    To sober myself. Are the doors bolted?

DELANEY   They are. All's dark as a hearse-cloth
    In St Augustine's. I stopped the key-holes
        With rags.
    (*chuckling*)
                                When you codded the crowd
    That day, play-acting on Essex Quay, Sir,
        An' the tin whistles an' crowders

Were jeered in the gutter by butties an' gutties
    An' not a make in their mugs,
I nearly jacksed my wipe-gut
    With laughing to see long mugs

Outside in the rain at the public-houses
    With divil a hope of naggin
Or pint, their droopy moustaches an' cat-licks,
    As they cutaway'd home to be nagged.

McGUCKIN   You have another laugh coming, Delaney.
    It's part of my bet, but mum's
The word. It will liven up Liberty Lane.

DELANEY   Is it strawmen, Sir?

McGUCKIN   No.
                        Mummers.

(He picks up blackthorn stick. Lights dim as he comes forward, groping, into spotlight. Vague figures gather in background.)

'ZOZIMUS'   Gather round me, Boys, for well you know
     St Patrick was born in Bull Alley.
Some say your man was Taffy, the so-an'-so,
     But that, Boys, is up my Ball Alley.

     Am I standin' in wet or a paviour's puddle?

VOICES   On dry land, Zozimus.

'ZOZIMUS'
     I'm not, ye desaivers, I'm swimming the Poddle.
       If I go down a manhole, I'll moslem
     The lot of youz, string up your black-an'-white
           puddings
     An' sausages.

VOICES   Don't squeeze your lemon.
     But give us sweet word of St Mary,
They called the whoor of Jerusalem,
     How she varted,
             An' sold her mare's tail

For a luvely pot of balsam.

'ZOZIMUS'   Will you wait
     Till I scratch myself under the oxter?
Do you think I'm a Pro-Cathedral waite,
     The blessed donkey or the ox?

VOICES   Sing *Pharaoh's Daughter*
                  Prodigal
   Son
     Strike up, Zozimus.

'ZOZIMUS'   Go long to Hell with all Protestants.
      An' may we never simmer.

    I'll tell you now of Dirty Dick
        An' swipe them orange fellas
    With their Antient Concert Rooms, their dickies
        An' college ducks an' umbrellas.
    (tin whistle as he recites)
    At the dirty end of Dirty Lane
    Liv'd a dirty cobbler, Dick Maclane;
    His wife was, in the old King's reign,
        A stout brave orange-woman.

    On Essex Bridge she strained her throat,
    And six-a-penny was her note.
    But Dickey wore a bran' new coat,
        He got among the yeomen.

    He was a bigot, like his clan
    And in the streets he wildly sang
    O Roly, toly, toly, raid, with his old jade.

    (enter the real Zozimus)

VOICE (truculent)
    I'm a Proddy.

VOICES   Then be St Balize's disease
      An' his holy flannel, I'll poke out
    Your swollen tonsils.
                    I'll chapel-o'-blaze you
    An' expose your hoky-poky.

'ZOZIMUS'   Be cripes, you won't, you straw-foots, you big
      Galoots. He's a Dublin man
    Like myself.
                    Shake hands, Sir.

                                        Them bigots
            Were never emancipated.

ZOZIMUS   Men and women, who's that imposterer?

VOICE   Zozimus, himself, Sir.

ZOZIMUS   Are you seein' my double?
                              Sure, he's taken my posture
            An' stolen my songs an' hymns.

        Come, Boys, grasp his posteriors,
            The scruff of his neck, an' pitch him
        Into the Liffey or I'll bate the posthumous
            Out of him on my pitch here.

        Don't you know he's really Beelzebub,
            That fly-god, an' he's got you
        By it, an' your daughters by the bub
            For his name is the Unbegotten?

'ZOZIMUS'
        Don't mind that foul-mouthed blackguard, Boys.
            He stinks like Anna Liffey
        An' his language is all blague —
            But I'll blacken his analectas!

        Come on, you unsunned Cimmerian,
            Though you're not dimensional,
        I'll take you on with your Mary Anne,
            Her tail an' what I won't mention.

        (*Zozimus and his rival contend silently with sticks.
        The effect is uncanny. Lights dim, leaving them in the
        spotlight.*)

20

DELANEY (*to McGuckin*)
    By all the holy Mysteries,
      They're not Dublin men
    At all. So we'd better be scooting, Mister.
      Them's ghosts an' we're seein' double.
    (*Zozimus and crowd fade out. Lights up. Loud knocking. McGuckin lowers a drink.*)
    The doss, quick.
              Those droners'll need a stiff one
    An' if they get wind of your play-acting
    They'll want a real wake and yourself as the Stiff
      For nothing less will please them.

(*He opens door and the Ballad Singers enter. He moves candle to end of side-shelf, leaving 'Zozimus', now in bed, in the shadow.*)

KEARNEY   Is he bad?

DELANEY   He couldn't be worse, man.
    His toes are turning up,
    His head rolling round like a mangol-wurzel
      An' he's newly at the turnpike.

KEARNEY (*at bedside*)
    Cheer up, my aul' Geranium;
      No better clay's in pot.
    Your bud will redden an' bloom in the rain
      Though you're paler than poteen now.

'ZOZIMUS' (*cheerfully*)
    You're right. I'll chew my quid o' baccy,
      Pinch snuff an' quit my moaning.
    Your hand, Kearney, and may Bacchus, not
      Vartumnus, possess Pomona.

O'LEARY   Cheer up, like us, you'll be well-lit
        To-night, my aul' Gasoleer, an'
   Your recitations won't be littered
        For a long time yet.

'ZOZIMUS'   That's O'Leary.

O'LEARY   Cheer up, my aul' Segochia. You're good
        For many another Lent.
   An' no descendants will scatter your goods
        Till you get back all you lent

   To those bummers down in Clanbrassil Street.

'ZOZIMUS'   That's so.

MAGRANE   An' I've come here to recite
   Those ballads bright as the brassy knobs
        Of your double-bed — a sight

   You've never seen — when I'm well-oiled,
        And your songs like Sesame,
   Lovely an' yellow as its oil
        'An' gayer than foxglove,' sez Sammy

   My friend —

'ZOZIMUS'   Magrane.

MAGRANE   You'll warm the bed-sheets
   Till your flowers o' speech are cut down
   By time, declare bold words from your broad-sheets
        Like Emmet in the wood-cut.

'ZOZIMUS'   Start up the wake for my living corpse
        An' vigilate the Nation
   Before the white-an'-red corpuscles
        Are cold and my last carnations

22

Shed, for I'll stay, my fingers, in the pink
    An' tell of untarnished
Wreath of amaranth, pansy, pink,
    Till I come to my tarnation.

(*Crowd of men and women with bottles enter. Some women go respectfully to the bed.*)

DELANEY   Come all ye, men an' women, fill up
    Your cans with a rozimer
An' give our Zozimus a fillip
    Before he goes.

               The rosin's for

The fiddlers till they've done their accompaniments
    An' if annie interrupts
Their b's an' f's, the Boys will encumber
    The back-lane with rupture-belts.

HUMPY SODLUM
    An' after the ballads, we'll dowse the dips,
        Play *Hunkering*

GORT WHELAN   An' *Cutchee-coo*

COLLEEN OGE
    An' *Croppies Lie Down* when you're feeling dippy.

HUMPY SODLUM   Yes, Girls, an' *Fan-me-Cool.*

BILLY BOLAND   With *Wind up the Tick-tock*

GORT WHELAN   An' *Hic Haec Hoc*

MRS LISA BOLAND   An' *How's your Cockalorum.*

HUMPY SODLUM
    Girls, knock your cups back till you hiccupped
        An' beware o' the Marrion Cocklers.

(more guests arrive)

MRS FLAHERTY
      Mrs Hannigan, did you ever see the like
        Of that in a Christianised land,
      Those dressed-up hussies, them ikey wans?

MRS HANNIGAN   I've seen a lot from the landing
      Winda: young wans an' fellas hugging
        An' mugging, but to escort
      Them lassies here — ask Mrs Huggins —
        Is terrible. I'd scorch

      Their fal-de-lals.

MRS FLAHERTY   To think of street-walkers
        In this respectable place.
      They should be working in Walkingstown
        At the mill, not taking the place

      Of their betters.

MRS HANNIGAN   The wonder-working Franciscan,
        Who preaches Hell-fire to the say-gulls
      An' all of them other Cispontines
        Should be told. He'd have a say

      In the matter.

MRS FLAHERTY   Aye, Father Sulpicius
        Would deal with their sins of occasion
      An' frighten them like the pis-skators
        Who pull out their big eels on the Quay.

MRS HANNIGAN
      You're right, ma'am, all brazen-faced wall-pushers
        From the red-hot Kipps of Mabbot Street,
      Short-timers in doorways at Ussher Island.
        There's Blanketty May and Peony Mab.

      An'—

THE TOUCHER MAGUIRE
> Did youz never hear tell o' Saint Mary,
>> The Whoor of Jerusalem,
> With her luvely buzzom, the night-mare
>> Of christianers.

MRS FLAHERTY (*to the Toucher*)　Lemmy
> Go!

THE TOUCHER MAGUIRE
> Jewmen, the infidel Moor,
>> Sure when they had clapped an
> Eye on her handy behind, Mrs Moore,
>> She poxed them, she soft-sored, she clapped them.

> But, Zozimus, the Bishop, convarted
>> The Whoor o' the East, baptised
> And wet her all over in gallons of Vartry
>> Till his holy volume capsised her.

CHORUS　Till his holy volume capsised her.

THE TOUCHER MAGUIRE
> She gave the crabs to the nuns in her convent
>> And they sent her out to buy blackwash,
> For they found them very inconvanient,
>> But she stopped to pray with a black-man

> An' left the Sisters of Mercy to scratch
>> Themselves an' when she returned the
> Next week, she kept them up to the scratch
>> An' they had to turn her out

> In tears with her fare to Constantinople.
>> So she gave them her boils, but
> Before she could get to the Consulate there,
>> The Turcos redipped an' boiled her.

CHORUS   The Turcos redipped an' boiled her.

NOBS FAHY
    An' she wasn't the worst. The King o' the Beggars,
      Bold Dan O'Connell, sure he fathered
    The half of us all from Kilbeggan
      An' Birr to Puck Fair.

PHELIM BRADY (*menacing*)   Whisht, Fahy!

NOBS FAHY   Sure, he's famous for his hortations
      An' nobody can deny it.
    An' he'd bate King David when he was hoary
      Yet always nigh it in his pavilion.

PHELIM BRADY   By the blessed mumps
    Of St Blaise, I'll make you a tenor.

NOBS FAHY   Get back, you cut-purse.
                                I'll mummify
    Your lights at Tenebrae.

FRED FURY (*in corner*)
    Sure they say he's infatuated
      With a lassie who won't be converted.

NOBS FAHY   That's true.

PHELIM BRADY   Ah dip it in fat, chew, ate it!

NOBS FAHY   He's a hard chaw, Dan O'Connell.

THE TOUCHER MAGUIRE
    Don't mind them, Mrs Hannigan. They're
      Trying to badger you, an'
    Get up your dander. But I'll hand it to
      You, if you're feeling that bad

By the Back o' the Pipes at eleven
    To-night with due respects,
If you'd like a bit of levitation.
    But you'd better put on your specs!

MRS HANNIGAN   Get along, you smutty Corkonian,
    You want all the works for nowt.
I'll pepper-pot your polonio.

MIKE MYLER   Eh, ma'am, I'll lend you my knout.

MRS HANNIGAN
    You Cossack.

BRIAN O'LYNN   Ah, leave the woman to her sheeny
    And mind the rip in your pants or
Some Colleen Oge will dish your drisheens
    When you've warmed up the cooking-pan.

So, back to Coal Quay, my shandy-gaffer.

THE TOUCHER MAGUIRE
    I'll not. I've paid my corkage.

(*peal of bells*)

BRIAN O'LYNN   The window-breaking Bells of Shandon
    Have just come up from Cork.

(*Delaney intervenes*)

DELANEY   Now for Come-all-ye's, Entertainments,
    So go steady with the booze
My Boys. Don't guinness your containers
    For we don't want any boos.

BIG JIM PLANT   Pat has a half-nelson up his sleeve
    To give us all a start,
I've seen him peel his biceps, the sleeveen.
    We're waiting, Pat, so start.

(Two of my great-grandfathers come in)

DELANEY   Will you look who's here!
                                    Mr William Browne
    Who owns the tannery in Watling Street.
    (chuckling)
                                    He does them brown
    With ballads, bitter as tannin —

Those victuallers and vintners, flour-an'-salt merchants
    Of Thomas Street and the Cornmarket,
Not to speak of haberdasherers, robbing mercers,
    With his scorching words and remarks.

All know he's the friend of ballad-makers
    An' slips each a silver crown
To sing him songs at their shop-doors for make
    An' wing from the nudgy crowds.

I came in to greet you for I heard a great sound
    As I passed by with Dennis Clarke
So good evening to you, all and sundry.
    He's my confidential clerk.

CLARKE
    One of the Clarkes from Black Ditches, Blessington.

MR BROWNE *(lowering voice)*
    I'm told the bard's on his sick-bed
    Since Monday. We'd like to have his blessing —

CLARKE   Though we hear no sweep o' the sickle

(they go over to bed)

DELANEY   An' now we're having some grand new ballads
    For our visitors.
                        Kearney:

VOICE   Spifflicated.

DELANEY   O'Leary, my Lad!

VOICE   Paralytic.

DELANEY   The Meathman:

VOICE   Canned.

VOICE   They're all of them langers.

VOICE   Yewerinated.

DELANEY   Ah! potes will be potes.
     So Mr William Browne, you're in.
        That liquor was too potent,
     Now one of your ballads.

MR BROWNE   Here's a broad-sheet
        I picked up at Skinners Row.
     The language in it? Well, rather broad.
     (*Clarke whispers to him*)
        Sorry, I found it near Roe's

     Distillery — so don't tell the Missus.

CROWD   We'll swear on a sack of Bibles, Sir,
     Or take the pledge from the missioner
        Although we are fond of imbibing.

     (*Tin whistle. He recites in the traditional manner.*)

MR BROWNE   As I went up their Nelson's Pillar
        The steps went round and round,
     An' who should come down them but Lady Sackville!
        An' her drawers were coming down, too, My Boys.

CHORUS   Her drawers were coming down, too.

MR BROWNE
 'The string of me whatnots is broken entirely'
  Sez she, an' her luk was a sly wan.
 'Would you like to see a fine pair o' legs,
  Young man?' But I turned the blind eye, My Boys.

CHORUS An' he winked with the seeing wan.

MR BROWNE
 She pulled up her skirt to fasten the doings,
  'It's a very large size,'
 Sez she, when I gave her a helping hand,
  'An' you tuk me by surprise, My Boy.'

CHORUS He tuk her by surprise.

MR BROWNE As we came down from Nelson's Pillar
  She thanked me for my trouble.
 'We'll meet again,' sez she, 'in the Lar
  Above the streets of Dublin, My Boy.'

CHORUS Above the streets of Dublin.

  (*Applause. He goes aside with Delaney.*)

MR BROWNE How do you like the bran' new wig
  I bought last week for Ascot?

DELANEY It's black as a bag of coal from Wigan!
  That's best for nuts. Though if you ask

 Me, Bill, I like the pepper-an'-salt one
  An' the other, a natty nasturtium,
 You sported that time you won
  A packet at the Gran' National.

MR BROWNE If my wife buys a new Dolly Varden,
  I wear a lighter toupée
 For there's nothing like variety
  Whenever there's debts to pay.

30

I've one for every day in the week
  And each of them makes me cheerful.
Sure, the wigmaker knows my little weakness
  So here's to your very good cheer!

(*They drink. He slips a few sovereigns to him.*)

A special contribution.

DELANEY   Two golyons!
  (*goes to bed*)
Zozimus, feel an' bite them,
My angeshoir.

'ZOZIMUS' (*to Mr Browne*)
                    By your goloshes,
My gallstones an' the last bite
O' bread, Mr Browne, I can digest
  In my latter solitude,
My thanks.
              We'll spend then on fun and jest
Before the clergy call my tune.

(*My two great-grandfathers leave*)

DELANEY   We're slipping out for more of the hard tack.
  So don't wake the invalid.
His gizzard has had a dire attack.
  We'll send for a leading physician.

(*He leaves with some others. General merriment,
fiddlers start to play. Brian O'Lynn and Mollie Malone
dance a jig.*)

BIG JIM PLANT   Whack, fol-the-diddle O, the diddle O!

MRS MULLIGAN   Arrah, fol-de-rol, the titty O!

BIG JIM PLANT   Sure, they say, my dear Mrs Mulligan,
        It's the Pride of the Coombe;
And that's the spot where we all began
        Our first wee sup with a coo, my Boys.

(They whirl with the other couple into a four-handed reel.)

CURTAIN

ACT TWO

(Wild merriment. Delaney and others enter with more drink. He claps for silence. Fiddles and tin whistles start. Brian O'Lynn and Mollie Malone mime as Delaney recites a ballad of the time.)

DELANEY   Oh! 'Twas Dermot O'Nolan McFigg
     That could properly handle a twig.
         He went to the Fair
         And kicked up a dust there,
     In dancing the Donnybrook Jig
         With his twig.
     Oh! My blessing to Dermot McFigg!

     The souls they came crowding in fast,
     To dance while the leather would last,
         For the Thomas Street brogue,
         Was there much in vogue,
     And off with a brogue the joke passes,
         Quite fast,
     While the cash and the whiskey did last.

     But Dermot, his mind on love bent,
     In search of his sweetheart he went,
         Peeped in here and there
         As he walked thro' the Fair,
     And took a small taste in each tent,
         As he went.
     Och! on whiskey and Love he was bent

     And who should he spy in a jig,
     With a Meal-man so tall and so big,
         But his own darling Kate
         So gay and so neat;

Faith, her partner he hit him a dig
  The pig,
He beat the meal out of his wig!

Then Dermot, with conquest elate,
Came up to his beautiful Kate;
  'Arrah! Katty,' says he,
  'My own cushlamacree
Sure the world for Beauty you beat,
  complete,
So we'll just take a dance while we wait.'

The Piper, to keep him in tune,
Struck up a gay lilt very soon,
  Until an arch wag
  Cut a hole in his bag,
And at once put an end to the tune
  Too soon.
Oh! the music flew up to the moon.

To the Fiddler says Dermot McFigg,
'If you'll please to play "Sheela na gig",
  We'll shake a loose toe
  While you humour the bow.
To be sure you must warm the wig
  Of McFigg,
While he's dancing a neat Irish Jig!'

(Delaney addresses the crowd)

DELANEY   This is the first centenary
           Of that great patriot
        Dean Swift, who died in eighteen-hundred
           An' forty-five. Pay-roll

34

An' bribe was scorned by our noble Drapier.
    He dipped an' raised his pen.
All England shook; for he tumbled the drays
    An' cartloads of Wood's pence.

The Quality have forgotten his toil
    But the Coombe Boys still remember,
While ladies grimace at toilet table,
    They bless him on Ember Day.

He wrote a pome for Webster, tailor,
    Who abided in Weaver Square,
When times were bad in the retail trade.

FRED FURY   He was always on the square.

It's a pageant of famous charácters
(*cheers*) An' regardless of great cost
We present the march-by of our actors
    Arranged in Liberty Costumes.

Come all ye, industrious Huguenots
    With your wonderful frieze
That has never snapped a threadknot
    Although you eat fries on a Friday.

DAN KENNY   Some say the pathriotic Dane
    Enjoyed two mutton chops
Of fast-days, though he was clean-shaven
    An' had no mutton chops!

(*'Zozimus' sits up, blankets around him and recites in
clear English*)

'ZOZIMUS'   AN EPILOGUE BY DEAN SWIFT

Who dares affirm this is no pious Age,
When Charity begins to tread the Stage?
When Actors, who at best, are hardly savers,
Will give a Night of Benefit to weavers?

Stay — let me see, how finely will it sound!
Imprimis, from his Grace an Hundred Pound,
Peers, Clergy, Gentry, all are Benefactors;
And then comes in the *Item* of the Actors.
Item, the Actors freely gave a day —
The Poet had no more, who made the Play:
(*The Actors line up in costume and come forward in turn*)
But whence this wondrous Charity in Players?
They learned it not at Sermons, or at Prayer:
Under the Rose, since here are none but Friends,
(To own the Truth) we have some Private Ends.
Since Waiting-Women, like exacting Jades,
Hold up the Prices of their old Brocades;
Well-dressed in Manufactures here at Home,
Equip our Kings and Generals at the Coombe.
We'll rig in Meath Street Aegypt's haughty Queen
And Anthony shall court her in Rateen,
In blue shalloon shall Hannibal be clad,
And Scipio trail an Irish plaid.
In drugget drest, of Thirteen Pence a Yard,
See Philip's Son amidst his Persian Guard.
And Proud Roxana fired with jealous Rage,
With fifty Yards of Crape shall sweep the Stage.
(*She whirls, unrolling the crape, then stops, half clad and dashes off.*)
In short, our Kings and Princesses within,
Are all resolved the Project to begin;
And you, our Subjects, when you have resort,
Must imitate the Fashion of the Court.

(*The Actors parade, march off. Conversation.*)

36

DELANEY   We now present *O'Rourke's Great Feast*
With all the props an' effects.
The wash of its drink would have choked the gratings
If they'd any.

DANNY BOY   Sure, Dane Swift fecked
That song from the Irish.

DERBY DOYLE   Two hussies came
From England, dressed in their best
To nobble him but he soon hustled
An' bustled that pair o' besters.

NED FLYNN   But what did these shinannikers want from
The Dane?

DERBY DOYLE (*lowering voice*)
A touch o' the relic.

NED FLYNN   Why didn't he marry the wealthier wan
An' leave his relict?

The rhino?

DANIEL O'ROURKE   Them black Prodistants say
Our relics are only diварsions.

DERBY DOYLE   Will some-wan give that bostoon a prod?

DELANEY (*impatient*)
This is a longer version.

(*He brings a drink to 'Zozimus', general amusement.
Fiddle and tin whistle, actors enter, speak and mime
in spotlight. Crowds in dark, down stage.*)

'ZOZIMUS' (*narrating*)
Let O'Rourke's great feast be remembered by those
Who were at it, are gone, or not yet begotten.
A hundred and forty hogs, heifers and ewes

Were basting each plentiful day and gallons of pot-still
Poured folderols into mugs. Unmarried
And married were gathering early for pleasure and
  sport.

ACTORS (*speaking and miming*)
 'Your clay pipe is broken.'
        'My pocket picked.'
            'Your hat
Has been stolen.'
     'My breeches lost.'
         'Look at my skirt torn.'
'And where are those fellows who went half under
  my mantle
And burst my two garters?'
       'Sure, no one's the wiser.'
'Strike up the strings again.'
       'Play us a planxty.'
'My snuff-box, Annie, and now a double sizer.'

'ZOZIMUS'
 Men, women, unmugged upon the feather-beds,
 Snored until they heard the round clap, the step-dance
 Again, jumped up, forgot to bless their foreheads
 And jigging, cross-reeling from partner to
        partner, they trampled
 With nail in brogue that cut the floor to shavings.
 'A health, long life to you, Loughlin O'Hennigan.'
 'Come, by my hand, I'll sing it in your favour,
 You're dancing well, Marcella Gridigan.'

(*A spotlight shows floor with a couple going to bed.*)

ACTORS 'A bowl, Mother, and drink it to the last drop'
 Then came a big hole in the day.
       Light failed.

'Shake rushes for Annie and me, a blanket on top
And let us have a slap-and-nap of decent ale.'
Merciful Heaven, whoever saw such a big crowd
So drunk, the men with belt-knives of slashing,
     stabbing,
The women screaming, trying to hold up trousers
And others upon the table, twirling an oak-plant!
(more actors take part)
The Sons of O'Rourke came rolling from the doorway
In somersaults of glory. Bachelor boys
Were boasting, cudgelling more, more, more.
'My father built the monastery at Boyle . . .'
'The Earl of Kildare and Major Bellingham were
My . . .'
          'Sligo harbour, Galway, Carrick-drum-rusk.'
'And I was fostered . . .'
                    'Pull the alarum bell!'

(bell sounds)
'A blow for your elbow grease.'
                         'A kick in the bum.'
'Who gave the alarm?' demanded one of the clergy.
And swung his big stick — not as a censor.
Right, left, he plied it soundly to asperge them
In blood-drops, gave a dozen three more senses.
The friars got up with their cowhorn beads to haul
     him
Back, dust his habit.
                    Three Reverences tumbled
Into the ashes; Father Superior bawling
Until that congregation went deaf and dumb!
'While I was studying with His Holiness

And taking Roman orders by the score,
    Yiz sat on a settle with an old story-book,
All chawing roast potatoes at Sheemore.'

(*Lights up. General confusion, ructions, then silence
as Zozimus enters, striking out with his stick.*)

ZOZIMUS   Who's that imposterer ye're wakin';
        With Guinnesses an' doubles,
    Instead of me? Am I awake or
        Is my mind seeing double

    Since I heard the news in Smock Alley
        A while back?

DELANEY   It's Zozimus
    That's passing.

ZOZIMUS   It's down your alley alright
    To find my didymus.

    Have I no share in my own passing
        Or the dibs for the noddin' plumes
    And your collecting from passers-by?
        Don't I live by my holy plume?

    I've converted them wans in the tenements,
        An' magdalen'd the lot.
    Throw me my half-share o' the tin
        Or I'll uncify you all like Lot an'

    His pillar.

'ZOZIMUS' (*sitting up*)   He's the imposterer
        An' he wantin' my sacred death-dues.
    He's some play-actor who's taken my posture
        An' he'll razzle-dazzle with my jewels
    O' song.

ZOZIMUS   Boys, don't you know he's Moloch,
    The fish-god with only one fin,
    Who keeps the cod-banks an' covers his molluscs
      An' bosses the old Fin-nations?

'ZOZIMUS'   The name is Dagon, you ignoramus,
      An' I'm swimming the booty.

VOICES   Begod, we have two Zozimuses
('*Zozimus' jumps out of bed*)
    And both of them in their boots.

ZOZIMUS   He's changing to Vercingetorix.
    Where are you? (*striking out*)

VOICES   There
                      Beside you
   Where?
         Here

ZOZIMUS   Here
              He's a ventriloquist
    And he's turned my senses inside
 Out.

      God in heaven, have youz no pity
   On the blind man who tried to save youz
   All from the Everlastin' Pit
    An' get the Penny Savings

Bank to protect your wings?

MRS MULLIGAN (*moved*)   Hold back the
    Poor Jossers. They're long-lost twins.
  Their way is dark an' unbeholden
    An' their eyes have never twinkled.

(*A man at main door*)

MAN   Quick, men and women, the back-lane exit
        For the Hell-fire Franciscan
    Is striding the cobbles to make an example
        Of youz all to-night and fire

    Your tails, so keep them where they belong.
    (*watching from door*)
        He's running now with his skirts up.
    He's turning the corner of Long Lane
        An' he'll pull up your boards an' skirting.'

    (*Crowd rushes for the side-exit. Zozimus gropes for
    door followed by 'Zozimus'.*)

ZOZIMUS
    Wait for the Blind man. Are youz all decamping,
        Leaving me to his mercy
    An' Flaming Flowers?
                            Where's my aid-decamp?
        Am I to end up in Mercier's

    With splints in the Casualty Ward,
        Sitting up in a pose
    Of Plaster-o'-Paris? Is this my reward
        For a lifetime of composing?

    (*'Zozimus' pushes him out.*)

DELANEY (*winking at 'Zozimus'*)
    Come on. I'll guide you to the door
        For it's your only chance.
    He's not got your name in his dossier
        An' you'll not be in Chancery

    Before your napper has been boxed.
    (*to* 'Zozimus') There's whiskey to add to your diet
    On the shelf

42

'ZOZIMUS'   Give me that cash-box.

DELANEY   I won't.

'ZOZIMUS'   I'll make you the diet
        Of worms.

        (*Steps. He blows out candle, hurries to door.*)

'ZOZIMUS'   What's this?
                                My box of grease-paints.
            I've got you now. I'll careen
        Your bottom before I cut the painter
            So tell that to the Marines!

        (*Fr Sulpicius appears in moonlight at doorway.*)

FR SULPICIUS   Hide your misconduct, jereboams,
            In darkness, knowing your sins
        Have sent me. Hear my Placebo
            And kneel down, married, single.

        It is against the Bishops' ruling
            To hold a wake, put beads
        Aside. School-children know strap, cane, ruler,
            When Brothers lay bare obedience,

        Yet *Sacrilegia super defunctus*
            Is committed, to-night, by parents.

DELANEY   Father, we took no soup. Them Funkers
            Fled to their top-back pair

        O' rooms.

FR SULPICIUS   You came for a filthy purpose,
            Neglected religious duties,
        Insulted our Faith, my sacred stole,
            And never pay your dues:

43

Indulging in shameful practice
    And known abominations
Songs, games, that encourage lewd acts,
    Disgrace our Catholic nation.

DELANEY (*coming forward, servile*)
    'Twas only a spree for Tom Malone
        To warm his cockles with chat
    An' a few pints, poor twilight man
        For his teeth are chattering.

An' he couldn't say the Litany
    With us, your Reverence.
He felt so bad, we never lit any
    Candles for his two aul' grand-aunts

Crying their eyes out.
                I'll get the flint.

(*strikes in vain*)

FR SULPICIUS   What's wrong?

DELANEY   Be the sufferin' Jases —
    Excuse me, Father.
    (*showing tinder*) That mean aul' skinflint.
    It's worn out, an' I've no sulphur

Matches.
        I'll lead you to the poor old sod —
    I mean — the dying man.

FR SULPICIUS (*at bed*)
    Now try to tell your sins.

'ZOZIMUS' (*in low voice*)   Sodomy,
    Three rapes, man-slaughtering,
    An' fornication, seduction — when I'm sodden

For I'm Tom-any-Moll.
Notorious from Birr to Blacksod,
    See the mots an' animals run!
(half sitting)
Incest and other carnalities,
    Likewise necrophilism,
An' divers deeds of bestiality
    An' I've not had my fill, for

To-night, I'm going to commit murder —
    Martin McGuckin will freeze.
And they'll report this murky crime in
    To-morrow's *Freeman's Journal*.

Delaney, you've had two jokes, but this time
    Zozimus holds the Joker.

(getting up)

DELANEY   Holy St Francis, he's mad.

                                    Mind out, Father!

'ZOZIMUS'   He'd better.

                    This is the last joke.

(He tumbles out of bed, swinging stick, stumbling after
them as they rush out. Pause. Stage dims as he comes
forward into brightening spot.)

Come all ye, listen to my song.
    It's about a fair young maid —
Moryah — an' won't detain you long,
    For her bill was soon marked 'paid'.

In Egypt's land contagious to the Nile,
King Pharoah's daughter went to bathe in style.
She tuk her dip, then walked unto the land,
To dry her royal pelt she ran along the strand.

45

A bulrush tripped her, whereupon she saw
A smiling babby in a wad o' straw.
She tuk it up and said with accents mild
'Tare-an-ager', girls, which of yiz owns the chee-ild?

'Tare-an-agers' . . .

(*silence*)

        So, that's it.
                The very ghosts
Are absent.
        The Shakesperian O
Is surrounded by darkness.
                  It's time for me to go.
      The comedy is over.
(*dazed*)
But pray, who am I?
          Zozimus
Drunk?
      Or Martin, his man?
And who the Hell — for I must know —
      Is the Stage Manager?
(*slow steps*)
The ghost of Zozimus!

DELANEY (*returning*)   He's gone.

'ZOZIMUS'   That's not the right queue.

DELANEY
Well, then, he bottled his way through that scrum
  All roaring for a curer,

Ghost-pale. He slipped on a cabbage
  Stalk in the gutter outside.

46

A mot picked him up and the Boys are cabbing
    Him to the Meath. A side-car

Is rattling more paralytics on.

McGUCKIN (*taking off wig*)   Delaney,
    You devil, you'll get your money
And another fiver for the delay.
    My backers will settle on Monday.

DELANEY   We'd better skidaddle, Mr Martin
    McGuckin.

(*putting down stick*)

(*meaningly*)   His stick.
                    I'll close
The place up. Go by the Bird Market
    Or your jokes will soon be clovered.

I'll hide to-night from the Liberty Boys
    In the ruins of St Kevin's Abbey
Nearby. Those fellows will be boisterous
    An' rougher than the Abbots of

Missrule, you told me about, rampaging
    Before the High Altar, an' gargoyles
Grinning outside at Sins on the ramparts.
    But, first I'll have a gargle.
(*goes to table, tries bottles, mugs*)
Piss.
      Mother's ruin.
                  What's here?
                         A ball
O' malt?
      No, not one dram.

(*leaving*)   **A**
Notable conclusion to your balderdash!

(*McGuckin puts on wig, then slumps to the floor.*)

DELANEY (*at door calling*)
There's more to poetic drama.

(*Moonlight shines on prostrate figure. Spot dims.*)

SLOW CURTAIN

LIBERTY LANE by Austin Clarke is the twenty-seventh Dolmen Edition. The frontispiece, *The Ballad Singer* by Tate Adams, is printed from the artist's original wood-engraving. The book is designed by Liam Miller, set in Pilgrim type and printed and published at The Dolmen Press, North Richmond Street, Dublin 1, in the Republic of Ireland. Liam Browne saw the book through the press, and Jim Hughes composed the type which was machined by Garrett Doyle. This Dolmen Edition is limited to 500 copies.

February 1978.

Distributed in the U.S.A. and in Canada by Humanities Press Inc., 171 First Avenue, Atlantic Highlands, N.J. 07716.